CONTENTS

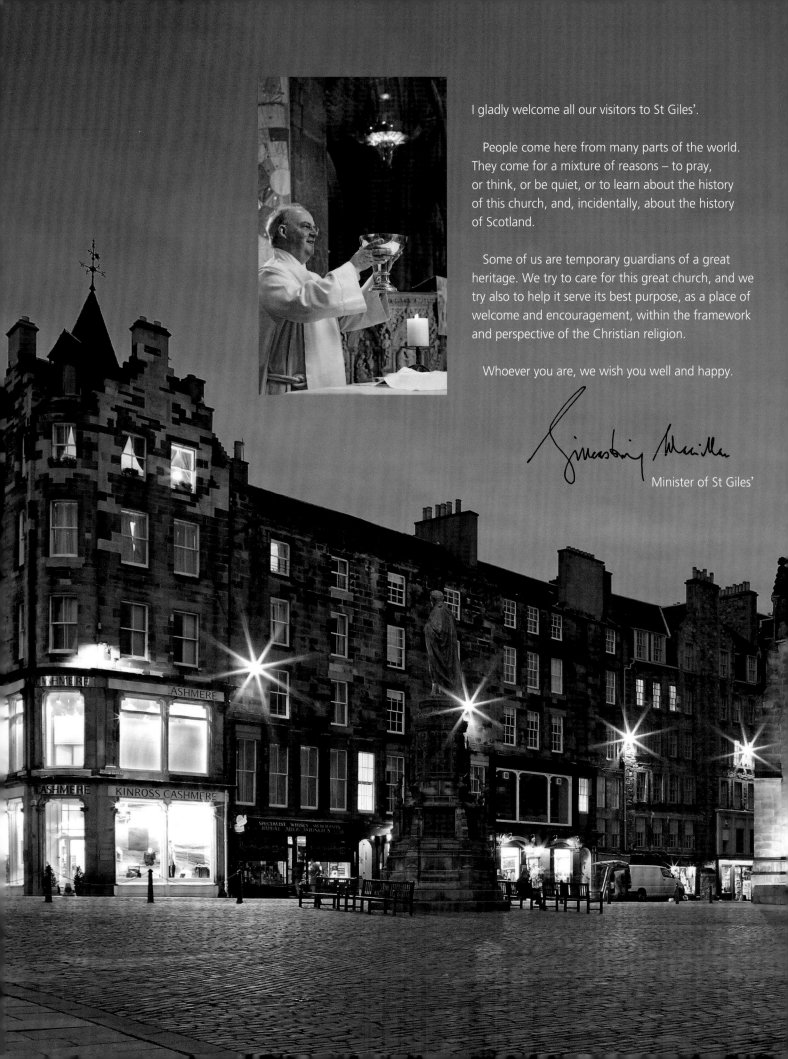

I gladly welcome all our visitors to St Giles'.

People come here from many parts of the world. They come for a mixture of reasons – to pray, or think, or be quiet, or to learn about the history of this church, and, incidentally, about the history of Scotland.

Some of us are temporary guardians of a great heritage. We try to care for this great church, and we try also to help it serve its best purpose, as a place of welcome and encouragement, within the framework and perspective of the Christian religion.

Whoever you are, we wish you well and happy.

Minister of St Giles'

A CHURCH IN THE BURGH
(12TH TO 15TH CENTURY)

Worshippers and visitors who come into St Giles' today are often enthralled by the spirituality of this space. From the first step they take inside, they are surrounded by a soft glow, by the subtle light shining through magnificently coloured windows and by a feeling of serenity and calmness – time and again a welcome change from the buzz and bustle of Edinburgh's Old Town outside.

At different times in St Giles' history, the pilgrim's eye would have been met by very different sights and a feeling of peacefulness might not have been the first thought to come to mind. A place of worship for nearly 900 years, the church has also faced war, fire and hatred. It has separated friends and re-joined enemies, welcomed kings and queens, soldiers, paupers, prisoners and judges. Most importantly, it has always been at the heart of Edinburgh and its moving history.

Early Christianity in Scotland is connected with the name of St Columba, who is often said to have brought it to Scotland and who certainly preached his faith in this country.

St Columba was born into a royal warrior family in Ireland in 521. From a very early age he was trained to become a priest, and during his missionary work in Ireland, he founded several monasteries. After an argument and, eventually, a bloody battle with the King, he was excommunicated and sent

1 Detail from the oriel window; the crest of a hart's head with a golden cross between the antlers recalls the legend of the foundation of Holyrood Abbey.
2 One of the few stones probably dating from the original Romanesque building
3 The Saint with a model of the church and the Seal of the Chapter of St Giles'
4 King David with a model of St Giles'
5 St Giles: he is commonly depicted with a hind and an arrow through his hand

4

away from Ireland in penance to convert as many people to Christianity as had been slain in the battle. In 563, he set foot on Iona in the west of Scotland and founded a monastery there – in the first place from which he could no longer see his native land. Iona became the centre for Christianity and missionary work in Scotland. Columba died there in 597.

When St Margaret (1045–1093) married King Malcolm of Scotland in 1070, she inspired the King and the court to follow her example and practice religious purity, integrity and spirituality. Better education for the court and improved care of the poor were indications of this change and a visible sign was the building of new churches.

Her youngest son, David, became King of Scotland in 1124 and it is believed that, in the early years of his reign, St Giles' was founded. At that time, Edinburgh seems to have been made into a royal burgh, and the legend of the foundation of Holyrood Abbey also falls into the same period.

The first stone church of St Giles' was probably built in around 1124. Following the Romanesque style, it would have had a chancel where prayers were read and mass was sung and a nave for the congregation. Not much is known about this initial building and only a few stones, including the top of a small pillar and several grotesque faces, have survived. They are set in the stonework now and can still be seen today.

The church was probably dedicated to St Giles from its foundation. It is said that St Giles (or *Aegidius* in Latin) was a prince born in Athens around 650. He went to France and became a hermit in the forests around Nîmes with a hind – a female deer – as his only companion. Legend has it that one day the King was hunting and aimed an arrow at the deer, which St Giles stopped with his hand. The hermit gained the respect of the King, who then built a monastery for him. St Giles was soon revered as the saint of

1

2

1 A Romanesque mask
2 A Romanesque grotesque
3 A consecration cross
4 St Andrew, patron saint of Scotland
5 St Andrew
6 View from the Chancel

3

| 1000 |
| 1100 |
| 1200 |
| 1300 |
| 1400 |
| 1500 |
| 1600 |
| 1700 |
| 1800 |
| 1900 |
| 2000 |

cripples and lepers. He died in France around 710. King David granted responsibility for the church to the religious order of the Lazarites whose chief purpose was to provide care for lepers.

The first recorded dedication of the church was carried out by Bishop David de Bernham in 1243. Two consecration crosses can still be seen in the building, but they probably date from later occasions.

The core of the building as it stands today most likely started taking shape after a fire in 1322 when a transept was possibly added to create the typical cross shape. The style in which churches were built had already changed from Romanesque to Gothic at that point. After a second fire in 1385, inflicted by the army of Richard II of England, the church was probably not too badly damaged, but a new impetus had been given for renovation work. It is from this time on that the first building records survive and chapels we still see today were built. By the time of the Reformation almost 200 years later the architectural structure of St Giles' probably looked very much as it does today.

During the later medieval period, prayers for the souls of the dead were of great importance to people

4

5

– the rich as much as the poor. For saying these prayers and for celebrating mass, altars were needed, as well as someone to conduct the services. Rich families might put an altar into the church for themselves only and pay clergy until literally the end of time to pray for their souls once they were dead. Other people could be part of a guild or even a confraternity and they also supported altars in churches. By the time of the Reformation, there were around 50 altars in St Giles', all dedicated to various saints and the Virgin Mary. Sometimes new chapels had to be built to provide space for new altars and this is one reason why churches expanded so much during this period.

The other reason why St Giles' grew so quickly was that the people of Edinburgh began to take pride in their town; having a bigger and more beautiful church was a welcome way to show their importance as a royal burgh. In 1466 the Pope granted St Giles' the enhanced status of a Collegiate Church, run by a dean (known as provost) and a chapter of canons (known as prebendaries). There was no bishop's chair in St Giles', but the new status was just one step below Cathedral status. St Giles' stayed a Collegiate Church until 1560 when, in the course of the Reformation, papal connections were officially severed.

From its foundation in 1124 until the union of the crowns in 1603, St Giles' always had links to the kings and queens of the time. During the seventeenth and eighteenth centuries, that interest was weakened, mainly because the monarchs were in London and rarely visited Scotland. In 1822, King George IV was the first monarch to visit St Giles' since the time of King Charles II, almost 200 years earlier. Since the last century, and especially since the Thistle Chapel was built in 1911, St Giles' has been regularly visited by the Sovereign and members of the Royal Family.

JOHN KNOX AND THE REFORMATION IN SCOTLAND (16TH CENTURY)

In the sixteenth century a change had come to Europe. People started to free themselves from the Catholic Church. The Reformation had started. Martin Luther pinned his 95 theses on the church door in Wittenberg in 1517. Soon after that, Ulrich Zwingli and then John Calvin started assembling and teaching like-minded people in Zurich and Geneva. One of Calvin's followers in Geneva was a Scot named John Knox.

John Knox was born near Haddington, a town about 20 miles (32 km) east of Edinburgh, around 1514. After receiving his primary education there, he went to the University of St Andrews to train as a (Catholic) priest and notary. Around 1544, Knox met George Wishart, an early Protestant reformer, and soon became one of his closest associates. This is probably when Knox converted to Protestantism. Wishart was burned at the stake for heresy in 1546, riots followed and, during these tumultuous times, Knox was taken prisoner and put in a French slave-galley. After rowing for 19 months in the galley, he was set free in France and made his way to the north of England, where he settled and became a well respected preacher. It was not safe for him to return to Scotland but England had become Protestant when King Henry VIII broke with Rome.

Times changed again after 1553, though, when Mary I became Queen of England and restored Catholicism. Knox fled to continental Europe where he continued his studies and teaching in Geneva and Frankfurt.

In 1559, when the religious climate in England changed yet once more and the Reformed faith was becoming increasingly influential in Scotland, Knox decided to return to his native country. He was soon to become the leading preacher in the Reformation. On 29th June 1559, he preached in St Giles' for the first time and only a week later he was elected minister. He stayed in this office for 13 years.

Queen Regent Mary of Guise – who had tried to uphold the Catholic Church – died in 1560 and, in the same year, Parliament passed acts to abolish Papal authority and to reform the church in Scotland. The country became officially Protestant and, when the Roman Catholic Queen Mary (usually referred to as Mary, Queen of Scots) returned from France in 1662, she did not interfere with the Protestant services but practised her religion in private. Remaining Catholics in Scotland were highly offended by her tolerance whereas John Knox condemned her for hearing mass and an array of other offences and regularly preached against her fiercely. According to his own account, when they met, Knox reduced the Queen to tears with his spiteful words and caustic remarks.

In 1567 Mary was forced to abdicate in favour of her infant son, James VI. In the following year, she fled Scotland only to be imprisoned and eventually executed in England. Scotland was ruled by Protestant regents until the King came of age, the Earl of Moray being the first until his assassination in 1570.

1

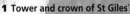

2

1 Tower and crown of St Giles'
2 Statue of John Knox by Pittendrigh Macgillivray 1903
3 Stone fragment; Knox became minister of St Giles' in 1559
4 Detail of Knox statue with Burne-Jones window in the background

3

JOHN KNOX 1559

1000
1100
1200
1300
1400
1500
1600
1700
1800
1900
2000

During John Knox's 13 years in St Giles', the interior of the church changed completely; furnishings were taken out and walls whitewashed; reminders of the old ways were sold or destroyed. Most noticeably, partition walls began to be put up to allow for congregations to assemble closer to the preacher to hear his sermons. The emphasis now lay more on the plain word and the Bible rather than on more elaborate forms of worship.

When John Knox died in 1572, Catholicism had been replaced by the Calvinist form of the Reformed faith, with an as yet incomplete form of the Presbyterian system of church government.

The Presbyterian system now current in Scotland is one of church courts. Each congregation is governed by its minister and a kirk session of elders elected from its members. Representatives from kirk sessions make up the local presbytery and once a year ministers and elders from all over Scotland meet as the General Assembly of the Church of Scotland to direct ecclesiastical policy.

James VI of Scotland also became King James I of England in 1603. The Church of England retained archbishops and bishops, following the Episcopal system of church government.

He favoured bishops because he believed they supported his position as monarch, and gradually reintroduced them into the Church of Scotland. He tried carefully to combine the Calvinist doctrine in Scotland with Episcopal practice. When his son, Charles I, became King in 1625 this careful approach was lost and a severe and bloody struggle started which dominated the next few decades. The Church of Scotland was not finally established until over a 100 years after Knox's death.

AFTER THE REFORMATION – RIOT, ROYALISTS AND REVOLUTION (17TH CENTURY)

Charles I became King in 1625 and eight years later he visited Edinburgh for his Scottish coronation. When he attended a service in St Giles', he already knew he would not be pleased with the plain Calvinist form of service and intended his own chaplains to take over and assume the service as soon as it had started. This was considered an affront and caused uproar amongst the people. Subsequently he tried to change the style of services altogether, starting to make them more similar to the way they were conducted in England. People were almost more upset by this than by the fact that he had set up a diocese in Edinburgh. St Giles' was now the seat of a bishop and Edinburgh, therefore, a city. By royal decree St Giles' had become a Cathedral.

In 1637, Charles I insisted on introducing a new prayer book. *The Book of Common Prayer* followed the content of the Anglican prayer book very closely even though it was written by the Scottish bishops. When it was first used in a service on Sunday 23 July 1637, legend has it that a woman called Jenny Geddes picked up her stool and threw it at Dean Hannay as soon as he started reading from the new book. This incident triggered events which led to the Bishops' Wars and, eventually, the Civil War.

In 1638, the National Covenant was signed, making the opposition to Charles I's involvement in church matters very clear. One of the statements of the document said in essence that Charles was the King of Scotland but that he was not the head of the Scottish church.

This Covenant – which took the form of a bond or agreement between the people and God – attracted the support of leading nobles such as James Graham, 1st Marquis of Montrose, and Archibald Campbell, 1st Marquis of Argyll. History brutally tore apart the harmony they had shown when both supported the National Covenant.

King Charles I was executed in 1649 at the climax of the Civil War and Oliver Cromwell arrived in Scotland in 1650. His second-in-command, John Lambert, had worshipped in St Giles' – soldiers and, on one occasion, even Cromwell himself, are said to have preached from the pulpit.

Montrose agreed with the Covenant as a means to take the power over the church from the Sovereign but he could not tolerate the execution of the King. Many Covenanters, though, did not make that distinction and simply opposed the King. Montrose was executed in 1650 and, although a Royalist, he referred to himself as a true Covenanter until the end.

1 Detail of 19th-century memorial to the Marquis of Montrose in the Chepman Aisle
2 Memorial plaque to Dean Hannay
3 Detail of the National Covenant
4 The Cutty Stool by Merilyn Smith
5 Plaque to commemorate the Jenny Geddes incident
6 St Eloi Aisle with the 19th-century memorial to the Marquis of Argyll

1000	
1100	
1200	
1300	
1400	
1500	
1600	
1700	
1800	
1900	
2000	

After the death of Cromwell it was decided to restore the monarchy, and Charles II came to the throne in 1660. Before long, Argyll – who had once crowned him with the Scottish crown in Scone in 1651 – was arrested by order of the King, tried for high treason in Edinburgh and sentenced to death for his collaboration with Cromwell's government. He was executed in May 1661. Argyll's head was placed on the same spike on the Tolbooth where that of Montrose had been displayed for over ten years. Only a few days before, Montrose had been given a magnificent funeral in St Giles' after his body had been reassembled – his arms and legs had been sent out to Stirling, Glasgow, Perth and Aberdeen to serve as a warning after his execution. Both men now have memorials in St Giles' – set up maybe as a gesture of reconciliation in the nineteenth century. After the Restoration, Episcopacy was reintroduced and the Covenanters were persecuted. A room in St Giles' known as Haddo's Hole was used as a prison during that cruel period.

When Charles II's brother and successor, James VII and II, revealed that he had converted to Catholicism, he was soon forced to abdicate by parliament in what is sometimes called the Glorious Revolution. He was succeeded by his Protestant daughter, Mary, and her husband, William of Orange. In an attempt to ensure their acceptance in Scotland, they supported the Scottish parliament in an act to secure the Presbyterian system of church government. The Church of Scotland as we know it today was finally instituted in 1690.

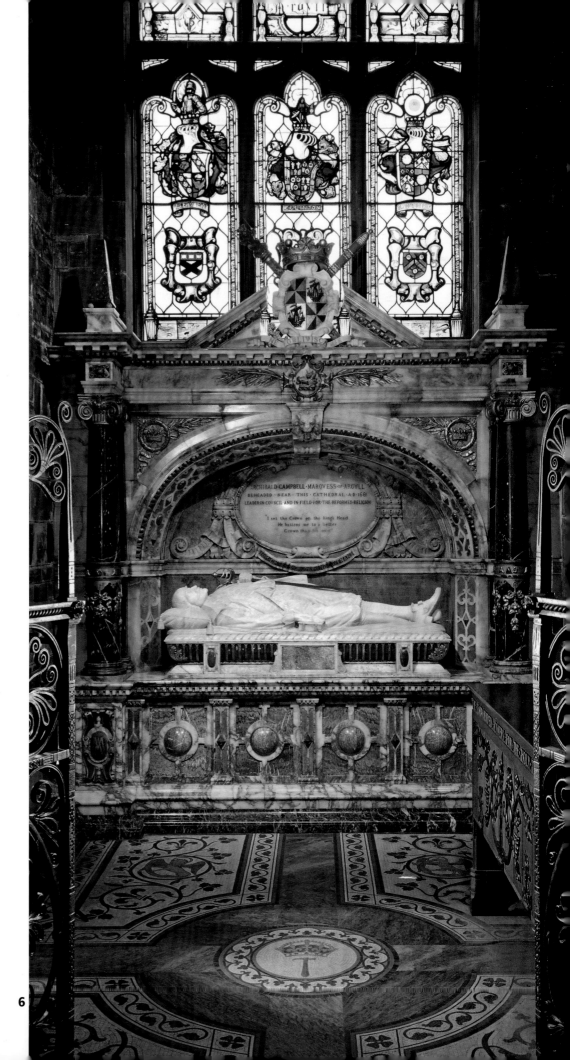

RESTORING ST GILES' (19TH CENTURY)

Tumultuous times during the Middle Ages, the Reformation and the seventeenth century were followed by a quiet period for St Giles' – both in religious development and architectural alterations to the building. This changed at the beginning of the nineteenth century.

Buildings around and partly even adjoining the church had been demolished to allow for more open space on the Royal Mile and Parliament Square. This included the Tolbooth where the prison was, and the Luckenbooths, which were small shops built against St Giles' walls. When the original church walls were visible again for the first time in many years, it became clear that they were leaning outwards and something would have to be done to prevent them from collapsing.

At the same time the inside of the church had long been divided by walls into different areas to enable different congregations and the General Assembly to meet. One part was even used as a police station. After money for the crucial repairs had been granted by the government, an architect was soon found and restoration work began in 1829. William Burn (1789–1870) had trained in

Edinburgh and London and is seen as a forerunner of the Scottish Baronial style. He was involved in the design of various churches and country houses and spent his later years in London, where he died.

Amongst his ideas to preserve the building and to bring some of its former beauty back was, most notably, the raising of the ceiling in the Nave and the Transepts to bring them in line with the original architecture of the Chancel and to put a focus on the cross shape of the Cathedral. Another measure he took was to prevent the collapse of the exterior walls by enclosing them in new sandstone. This still shapes the way St Giles' looks today. Looking at the outside of the church now, only the tower and the crown still show the original stonework.

The Burn Restoration was finished in 1833. Burn's actions may have destroyed and damaged much of the medieval fabric of the church, but they probably rescued it from deteriorating to a state too severe to be repaired again.

Whereas the first restoration was necessary to save the building, a second phase of restoration from 1872 to 1883 was aimed at unifying and beautifying the appearance of a building that was so central to Edinburgh and Scotland but so patched up and

1 Railing by Francis Skidmore
2 Memorial to William Chambers
3 The Angel Font is a replica of a font by Bertel Thorvaldsen in Copenhagen Cathedral. It was made by John Rhind and presented to St Giles' in 1883
4 Memorial to James Cameron Lees
5 Detail of the West Front by Rhind
6 St Giles' as seen from Parliament Square; all outside walls except the tower were enclosed in new sandstone in the 1830s
7 View from the Nave towards the Chancel

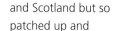

THIS CHAPEL IS IN MEMORY OF WILLIAM·CHAMBERS OF GLENORMISTON·LLD PUBLISHER LORD·PROVOST OF EDINBURGH·1865-69 TO·WHOSE·MUNIFICENCE SCOTLAND IS·INDEBTED·FOR·THE·COMPLETE RESTORATION·OF·THIS·ANCIENT CATHEDRAL·1883	1000 1100 1200 1300 1400 1500 1600 1700 1800 1900 2000

divided in its interior. The man who had the vision to create 'the Westminster Abbey of Scotland' was William Chambers.

William Chambers (1800–1883) was a printer and publisher. Together with his brother Robert he published periodicals like the *Gazetteer of Scotland*, the *Edinburgh Journal* and, in 1860, the famous *Chambers' Encyclopaedia*. In 1865 he was elected Lord Provost of Edinburgh and became a great benefactor who devoted himself to the restoration of St Giles'.

At his suggestion, the architect appointed was William Hay, a Scotsman who had spent most of his career in England and Canada. Hay had been involved in the design of many buildings in Newfoundland and in Toronto before returning to Scotland in the 1860s.

The main alterations to St Giles' during this restoration included taking down all the internal walls which had been put up to close off certain sections, in order to make the church one big space again, making the West Front more striking and fitting the church out with carved furnishings, such as a new pulpit and North Porch screen. The carvings were carried out by the Scottish sculptor John Rhind. New railings for many side aisles were made by Francis Skidmore, who was known as one of the best metalworkers in Britain.

The friendship and respect between Chambers and James Cameron Lees, who had been appointed minister of the Cathedral in 1877, gave another push to the restoration and by 1883 most of the work had been finished. Three days before the grand reopening service on 23 May, Chambers died.

After his death, his nephew Robert carried on supporting the church in efforts not yet accomplished, for example continuing to introduce more stained glass windows and encouraging the installation of monuments and memorials. Windows were put up in memory of William Chambers, his brother and his nephew, both called Robert, in the Chambers Aisle.

7

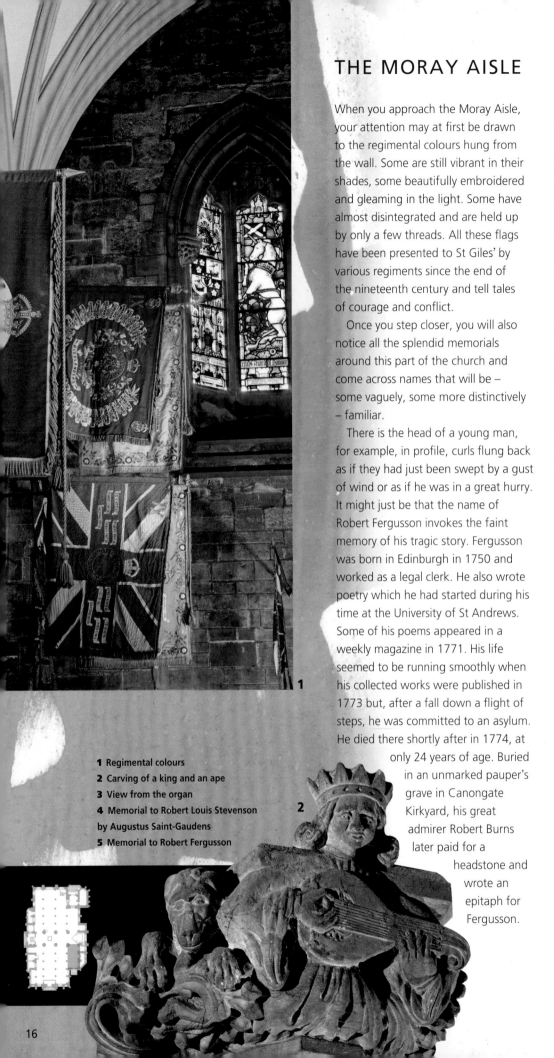

THE MORAY AISLE

When you approach the Moray Aisle, your attention may at first be drawn to the regimental colours hung from the wall. Some are still vibrant in their shades, some beautifully embroidered and gleaming in the light. Some have almost disintegrated and are held up by only a few threads. All these flags have been presented to St Giles' by various regiments since the end of the nineteenth century and tell tales of courage and conflict.

Once you step closer, you will also notice all the splendid memorials around this part of the church and come across names that will be – some vaguely, some more distinctively – familiar.

There is the head of a young man, for example, in profile, curls flung back as if they had just been swept by a gust of wind or as if he was in a great hurry. It might just be that the name of Robert Fergusson invokes the faint memory of his tragic story. Fergusson was born in Edinburgh in 1750 and worked as a legal clerk. He also wrote poetry which he had started during his time at the University of St Andrews. Some of his poems appeared in a weekly magazine in 1771. His life seemed to be running smoothly when his collected works were published in 1773 but, after a fall down a flight of steps, he was committed to an asylum. He died there shortly after in 1774, at only 24 years of age. Buried in an unmarked pauper's grave in Canongate Kirkyard, his great admirer Robert Burns later paid for a headstone and wrote an epitaph for Fergusson.

Just along the wall from Fergusson is the gilded profile of a woman, Margaret Oliphant, a nineteenth-century Scottish novelist. This plaque was actually unveiled by her friend J M Barrie, the creator of *Peter Pan*. Both plaques were made by the well-known Scottish sculptor, Pittendrigh Macgillivray, who also sculpted the statue of John Knox in St Giles'.

Further along is a strikingly simple tablet reading: 'Thank God for James Simpson's discovery of chloroform anaesthesia in 1847'. James Young Simpson (1811–1870) came from West Lothian, trained as a doctor in Edinburgh and carried out research into the relief of pain. After being appointed Professor of Midwifery at the University of Edinburgh, he also became physician to Queen Victoria. Best known for the discovery of chloroform as an anaesthetic in 1847, he introduced it as a means of easing pain during childbirth. Queen Victoria famously used chloroform when she gave birth to Prince Leopold in 1853, and after that it became more widely available. This plaque is one of many which links St Giles' with medical research and pioneers of medicine. Most of these memorials are located in the far north-east corner of the building.

On the west wall of this aisle is one of the great treasures of St Giles'. The bronze memorial to Robert Louis Stevenson (1850–1894) was created by the American sculptor, Augustus Saint-Gaudens, in 1904. The original sketch dates from 1888 and shows the author reading a newspaper and smoking a cigarette. The border is made of ivy. Stevenson, the celebrated Scottish author of such mesmerising stories as *Treasure Island* and *Dr Jekyll and Mr Hyde*, was born in Edinburgh and died in Samoa in the South Pacific Ocean. That same year Saint-Gaudens

1

2

1 Regimental colours
2 Carving of a king and an ape
3 View from the organ
4 Memorial to Robert Louis Stevenson by Augustus Saint-Gaudens
5 Memorial to Robert Fergusson

was asked to make a memorial to Stevenson for St Giles'. He adapted the design of the original for the Cathedral and the new version shows the author in the act of writing. The border is made of heather and hibiscus, linking the place where Stevenson was born with the place where he died.

The oriel or bay window in the recess above the Stevenson memorial was erected by The High Constables and Guard of Honour of Holyroodhouse in 1883. It shows the Royal Coat of Arms of Scotland, with the unicorn supporter, the Arms of the Duke of Hamilton, Hereditary Keeper of the Palace of Holyroodhouse, and a representation of the legend of the founding of Holyrood Abbey by David I.

The window next to it, showing biblical figures by C E Kempe, is in memory of John Ritchie Findlay, proprietor of the *Scotsman* newspaper in the late nineteenth century. He was a great benefactor and patron of the arts and presented Scotland with the Scottish National Portrait Gallery. The wooden pulpit in the Moray Aisle was a gift by him to St Giles'. It was designed by Sir Robert Rowand Anderson, who also designed the monument to the Marquis of Montrose in another part of the church.

Give us grace and strength
  to forbear and to persevere.
Give us courage and gaiety
  and the quiet mind,
Spare to us our friends,
Soften to us our enemies,
Bless us, if it may be,
In all our innocent endeavours.
If it may not,
Give us the strength to encounter
  that which is to come,
That we may be brave in peril,
Constant in tribulation,
Temperate in wrath,
And in all changes of fortune,
And down to the gates of death,
Loyal and loving to one another.

Robert Louis Stevenson

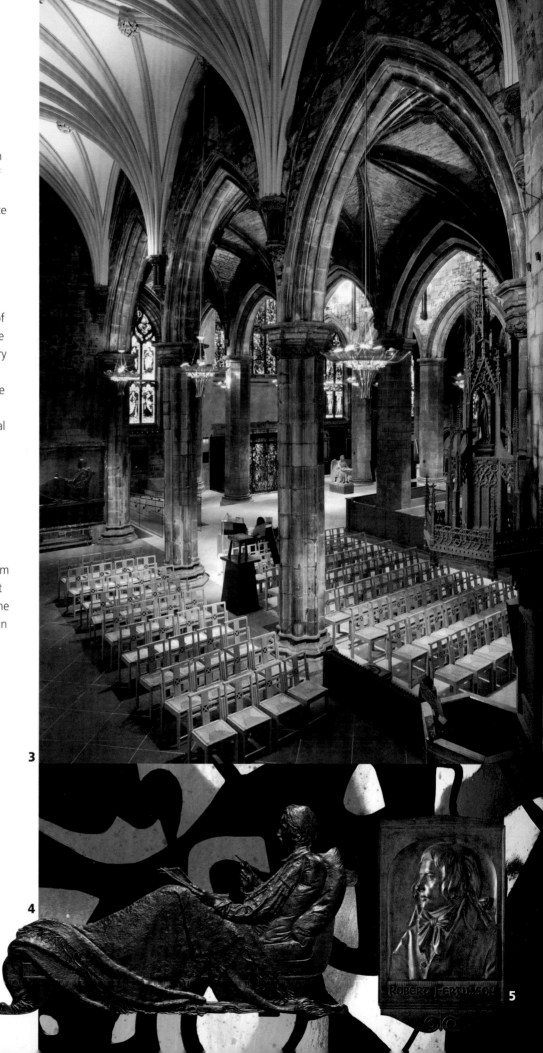

3

4

5

THE HOLY BLOOD AISLE

The harsh contrast between the comfort it offers at first glance and the story it tells at the second dominates this tiny aisle. The warm glow of candles, reflected from an old stone arch, is welcoming you. A little poem encourages you to light a candle and chairs invite you to rest for a while, think, pray.

The arch lit by the dancing flames on the back wall probably belonged to an altar close to this spot which was supported by the Confraternity of the Holy Blood in the Middle Ages. The Confraternity had been formed by the Merchant Guild in the early sixteenth century and its members had services held at the altar especially for them. When it was cleaned during the renewal programme in 2008, details of faces were discovered and carvings of symbols connected with Christ's passion – the Arma Christi – became more visible.

When you lift your eyes from the comforting glow, they are met by a forceful figure, preaching to a devastated-looking congregation, and by a man on horseback, eyes wide open in terror and hand on his chest, mortally wounded and hardly able to keep himself in the saddle.

1 and 5 Details of window depicting the assassination of the Earl of Moray
2 Detail of stone arch probably showing symbols of Christ's passion
3 Boss from the Nave ceiling
4 The Holy Blood Aisle

This historical window – one of the very few windows in the church that is not religiously themed – depicts the assassination of James Stewart, Earl of Moray, in 1570 and John Knox preaching at his funeral. The Earl of Moray was buried precisely here, at the foot of the steps, and the memorial on the right is dedicated to him; it was put up in 1879 as a replica of the one his wife Agnes, who was buried beside her husband, placed there after his death. The original memorial had been destroyed during the Burn Restoration around 1830 and only the brass inscription plaque remains of it.

Moray was a half-brother to Mary, Queen of Scots. After she arrived in Scotland in 1561, he was one of her main advisers but he eventually became her opponent. When she was forced to abdicate in favour of her young son, King James VI of Scotland, in 1567, Moray was the first of a number of regents ruling Scotland in his stead. He was a very important man, a protestant and a friend of John Knox. Moray was killed by one of Mary's followers in Linlithgow, shot with a gun from behind a window while riding down the main street. This was probably history's first recorded assassination committed with a gun. The window shows the moment when the gun has just been fired. You can see the weapon and a cloud of smoke still in the air in the top left-hand side section.

John Knox preached at his friend's funeral and Moray's wife, Agnes, is depicted mourning on the lower central panel. An interesting detail of the window is the attempt to show the interior of St Giles' during John Knox's times. The stained glass windows had been replaced and allowed a clear view to the other side of the street. It also gives an idea of how powerful and striking Knox must have been as a preacher.

5

MUSIC

The dark red organ in the South Transept is a prominent feature of St Giles'. Together with the choir stalls and the Sanctuary, it forms an axis of worship and music right through the core of the building.

The first organ to be installed in St Giles' since the Reformation was placed in the south-eastern corner of the building in 1878. The one you see today was made by Rieger Orgelbau from Austria and installed in 1992. It is – apart from three stops – a completely new instrument with mechanical action.

It has three manuals and 57 speaking stops, as well as a chromatic ring of 37 handbells cast in the Whitechapel foundry, which can be played from either the third manual or on the pedals. The striking case of stained Austrian oak was designed by Edinburgh architect Douglas Laird.

The Rieger organ has more than lived up to its reputation as one of the finest organs anywhere in the world. It has seen many concerts by internationally renowned players since its installation, and, most importantly, it has fulfilled the expectation that it should aid the encouragement of congregational singing and the accompaniment of choral music.

Records of choral music in St Giles' since the Reformation are hard to find. However, a choir of eight singers had been formed by 1879 and was soon augmented. The first organist since the Reformation, the 15-year-old John Hartley, had only been appointed a year earlier.

The choir originally sat on a raised platform in front of the organ, which, from 1909, was in a similar position in the South Transept to today's instrument.

The present choir is made up of 30 singers who provide the music for the two Sunday morning choral services: their repertoire is extensive, ranging from sixteenth-century Latin mass settings to music by contemporary composers.

Whilst the significant amount of music that the choir sings in its contribution to the worship in St Giles' is the raison d'être of its existence, they have been heard on many occasions over the years on radio and television, and make regular CD recordings. Since 2004 they have undertaken a number of foreign tours, visiting the USA, Canada, France and Greece.

The choir has existed in its present format of 30 experienced adult singers since 1962: it moved to its present choir stalls, south of the Crossing, in 1984. This position allows easy communication with the organ, even more so since the building of the magnificent instrument. The choir stalls were furnished with new music desks in 2009, completing the refurbishment of this area of the church.

St Giles' hosts a lively programme of musical events throughout the year, with concerts given by performers who come from many parts of Scotland and much further afield. Central to this concert activity is the weekly *St Giles' at Six* programme on Sunday evenings which hosts a variety of solo, chamber music and choral events. Many choirs from all over the world also give informal lunchtime concerts throughout the year.

Support is provided for many aspects of the musical life of the building through the work of the Friends of the Music of St Giles' Cathedral, founded in 2007.

1 A service at St Giles'
2 Detail of the 1992 Rieger organ
3 Detail of the organ
4 The choir during a service

THE CROSSING – SANCTUARY, TOWER AND THE NORTH WINDOW

A very much commented on detail in St Giles' is the position of the Holy Table right in the centre of the building. Most people would expect to find it at the east end, as is traditional in Cathedral architecture, and are somewhat startled to discover it elsewhere.

There are lucid reasons for this arrangement. The shape of St Giles' just lends itself to placing the Holy Table at the Crossing, where it was moved in 1981. Because the outline of St Giles' resembles a Greek cross rather than a Latin cross, the architectural heart, or centre of the building, lies where the Nave and Transepts meet. It just seems right also to move the central element of the church to this spot.

＋   **✝**

Greek Cross   **Latin Cross**

Probably more importantly, this position accords well with the atmosphere of a reformed church. Minister and people together surround the Holy Table. The beauty of this set-up really shows itself on a Sunday when bread and wine are shared in a big circle around the Communion Table, each serving the other.

The Sanctuary at the Crossing is believed to be the oldest part of St Giles', together with parts of the Chancel and the South Transept. The four sturdy pillars surrounding it date from the early fourteenth century. The banners with which they are decorated directly link the oldest part of the building with present-day worship. They have all been made with the help of members of the congregation and show, in a remarkable way, how to combine modern design with ancient stones. The colours of the banners – purple, green, red and white, gold and yellow – are changed according to the church seasons.

The brass lectern was presented to the church in 1886. The eagle is traditionally used on lecterns because it represents St John the Evangelist. The steps are a gift from the Normandy Veterans' Association.

Standing there and glancing up at the sun and stars painted on the old bell hole and shining down on the Holy Table, it is hard to believe that right above this spot is the Crown Steeple,

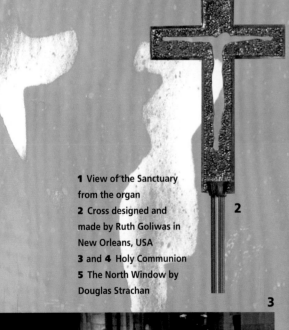

1 View of the Sanctuary from the organ
2 Cross designed and made by Ruth Goliwas in New Orleans, USA
3 and 4 Holy Communion
5 The North Window by Douglas Strachan

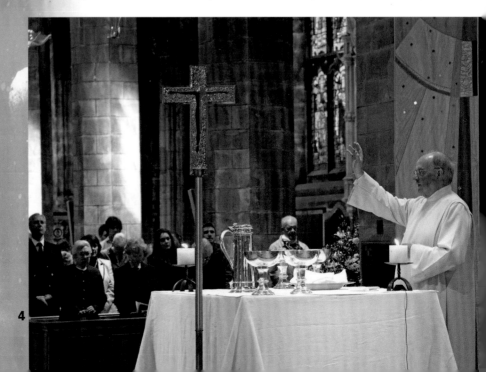

this landmark of the Royal Mile, the Old Town and even Edinburgh itself. Despite its modest height, the steeple can be seen from countless places in the city and from numerous roads leading towards it.

Around 1500, during the reign of James IV, the crown as we see it today was placed on top of the then existing tower. During John Knox's time, the old weathercock on top was replaced by a new copper one. About a hundred years later that had to be replaced as well; this is the one we still see today, after it was repaired and re-gilded in 1980.

Looking up to the tower from the outside you can see the only original late medieval stonework of the exterior building that is still visible. The rest of the building has been covered by a skin of new sandstone during the Burn Restoration in the first half of the nineteenth century.

As you stand near the lectern, you find yourself gazing at yet another magnificent work of art: the North Window. Portraying Jesus stilling the tempest, it was designed by Douglas Strachan, a Scottish artist from Aberdeenshire, in 1922 and was given by a merchant navy captain, Charles Taylor. It is a strikingly modern-looking piece in shades of green and blue and purple, combining to convey a dramatic image. The four big side panels show four archangels taming the gods of the winds – a very interesting parallel to the carvings of the heads of the four winds up on the crown looking out over Edinburgh. In the lower central panel a lamp, an anchor and a dove are hiding and, arching over all, is Noah's rainbow in the top panels. The colours are very intense: rough and violent during the tempest, calm and soothing in the still sea. It is always surprising how the window glows the way it does with no direct sunlight ever shining through it.

THE CHEPMAN AISLE
AND THE PRESTON AISLE

When you pass the organ, let your eyes be drawn to the splendid carving of a still, white marble figure set against a magnificent memorial. On a bright day, light creates a magical pattern of red, yellow and orange on the monument to the Marquis of Montrose. The illumination is created by a window which was installed in this aisle to remember his followers. The plaque below the window is to Sir William Hay of Delgaty, who was executed together with Montrose in 1650. To this day, flowers are frequently put on Montrose's monument by visitors from near and far who have a special connection with him.

'Scatter my ashes,
strew them in the air
Lord, since thou knowest where all
these atoms are....'
Lines on the Montrose memorial

The aisle takes its name from someone else, though, and there is a small but elaborate tablet to celebrate Walter Chepman on the chapel's west wall. Chepman is known to many as the person who introduced printing to Scotland, establishing the first Scottish printing firm, together with Andrew Myllar, in 1508, but he was also a rich merchant and a benefactor of St Giles'. He built this aisle in 1513, and he was buried here after his death in around 1528. During the Chambers' restoration in the nineteenth century, a carved boss with the arms of Walter Chepman and his first wife was found, as well as the carving of an eagle – the symbol of St John the Evangelist – to whom the aisle was first dedicated. Both carvings can now be seen high up on the ceiling of the aisle.

The larger chair below the Chepman memorial was presented to St Giles' by the Scottish Far East Prisoner of War Association in 1972 and the two smaller chairs were given to commemorate Mungo Park, a traveller and an explorer of the African continent. Born near Selkirk in the Scottish Borders in 1771, he died in Nigeria in 1806.

The area adjacent to the Chepman Aisle is called the Preston Aisle. It was built around 1460 as a special chapel

1 The coat of arms of Sir William Preston; the shield is held by two Green Men which can be seen in the background.
2 Fifteenth-century carving of an angel holding the Edinburgh burgh arms
3 The banners of the Knights of the Thistle
4 Montrose memorial in the Chepman Aisle
5 Memorial plaque to Walter Chepman
6 View of the Preston Aisle with the organ in the background

1000
1100
1200
1300
1400
1500
1600
1700
1800
1900
2000

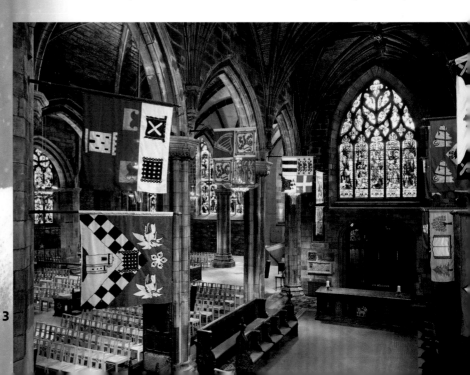

for an important relic which was acquired in France by Sir William Preston of Gorton in 1454: an arm bone of St Giles. The cult of relics was very important in the Middle Ages and owning this arm bone would have meant more pilgrims – and money – for the church.

The coat of arms of Sir William – a shield with the heads of three unicorns – is still visible in a few places on the superb ceiling and up on two pillars of the aisle. He was buried in a chapel to the east of the high altar, near the present stairs to the Lower Aisle. What happened to the arm bone of St Giles' after the Reformation is still a mystery.

In addition to the marvellous ceiling in the Preston Aisle, the colourful banners are the most prominent feature here. They belong to the Knights of the Thistle whose meeting place is the Thistle Chapel, its entrance glimpsed behind the iron gates at the east wall of the aisle.

On the same wall a few more rather interesting carvings can be found: a knight's grave marker from around 1200, the gravestone of Johannis de Touris de Innerleithen from before 1454, and one of the earliest carvings in stone of the arms of Edinburgh, in all likelihood dating from the fifteenth century.

The wooden Communion Table was designed by Robert Lorimer, who was the architect of the Thistle Chapel, and it once occupied the traditional spot at the east end of the Cathedral. When Queen Elizabeth II visited Scotland for the first time after her coronation in 1953, the Scottish Crown Jewels were presented to her at this table. For that occasion it had been enlarged. It has been in the Preston Aisle since the 1980s.

6

THE THISTLE CHAPEL

When you step down through the wrought-iron gates you find yourself in a low-ceilinged room, marvellously carved bosses looming closely over your head, heavy granite and green marble under your feet. On the walls there are rows and rows of dates and names of kings and queens, noblemen and simple knights. Through the black silhouette of the gates you still catch a glimpse of the colourful banners in the Preston Aisle and just before you is a high, narrow oak door, half open, inviting you to venture even further. What seems like a place steeped in history is actually the most modern addition to the structure of St Giles'. This neo-Gothic chapel was only built about 100 years ago, between 1909 and 1911, in less than two years.

You are in the Thistle Chapel, the spiritual home and meeting place of The Most Ancient and Most Noble Order of the Thistle.

The Order in its modern form was founded by James VII of Scotland (II of England) in 1687. He might have been reawakening a more ancient but dormant chivalric order, possibly dating back to the fifteenth or even to the early eighth century, but we cannot be certain about this. What we do know is that James VII – in a time of political uncertainty and turmoil – established the Order, probably as a means of securing the loyalty of his Council and the support of his Scottish subjects. When it was initiated, the meeting place chosen was Holyrood Abbey – next to the Palace of Holyroodhouse. The Order never met there though because, in 1688, the Abbey was destroyed during riots and James VII – a Catholic – had to abdicate and go into exile the following year.

Queen Anne finally established the Order in 1703. For over 200 years the Knights of the Thistle had no chapel, and meetings and installations were performed in other places. It was not until 1905 that the Earl of Leven and Melville donated money to restore the old Abbey chapel and create a set meeting place again. Restoring the chapel turned out to be impossible. Eventually it was decided to build a completely new one and to attach it to St Giles' Cathedral. The chapel was

1 St Andrew, patron saint of Scotland
2 The badge of the Order
3 and **4** A Knight's crest and the corresponding stallplate
5 View of the Knight's banners from the ante-chapel

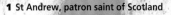

finished in 1911, and ever since the Knights have been meeting here at least once a year.

There are 16 Knights (and Ladies) of the Thistle and, in addition, a varying number of Royal members. The Sovereign is always the head of the Order and appoints new Knights. In addition to the Knights, the Order has officers who are the Chancellor, the Dean, the Usher of the Green Rod and the Secretary (the Lord Lyon King of Arms). Appointments only happen after a Knight has died. The announcement is normally made on St Andrew's Day, 30 November. The one fixed occasion when the Order meets each year is a service in the Thistle Chapel on St Andrew's Day or on the following Sunday. New Knights are usually installed by the Sovereign in a ceremony in the middle of summer.

Members of the Order are usually prominent Scots, or members of the Royal Family. The Sovereign alone decides who is appointed. Most members of the Order today come from a background of public service and distinct political, legal or cultural achievements. When they meet in the Thistle Chapel, they do so for a religious service conducted by their Dean. Being appointed a Knight of the Thistle is an honour only granted to very few distinguished people and one of the highest possible in Great Britain, second only to the Order of the Garter in England.

Apart from the stalls of the Sovereign and two members of the Royal Family, there are 16 stalls for the Knights and Ladies. On each one, the heraldic devices of its current holder are displayed: the coat of arms on the stallplate at the back of the seat and helm and crest on the top. The helm and crest are taken down on a Knight's death, but the stall plate with the coat of arms stays

5

in its position. As a result of this, all the Knights who have been members since 1911 are commemorated in the chapel (as are all the ones before that with their names in the ante-chapel). Early stall plates – from 1911 on – were enamelled by Phoebe Traquair, a celebrated artist of the Arts and Crafts movement.

The art of heraldry is still promoted in Scotland today. Only the Lord Lyon can authorise coats of arms and there are special artists who draw them. Some of the coats of arms used by Knights of the Thistle are inherited, but many of them are created especially for a particular person on becoming a Knight or Lady of the Order of the Thistle.

Even today it is still hard to believe that the whole chapel was built in only two years and that costs stayed slightly under the approved budget. Robert Lorimer (1864–1929), an outstanding Scottish architect and artist, was chosen as the architect. Very fond of the Scottish Baronial style and strongly influenced by the Arts and Crafts movement, he not only designed the Thistle Chapel but, in his later years, also the Scottish National War Memorial at Edinburgh Castle. He received a knighthood in 1911.

The artists and craftsmen employed in the building of the chapel and ante-chapel were amongst the finest and most skilled in Scotland at that time. Louis Deuchars made the models for both stone and wood carvings. The carving was mostly

carried out by Joseph Hayes in stone and William and Alexander Clow in wood. So much detail enriches this modest space that it could take hours to absorb everything. The faces of the angels playing musical instruments and holding heraldic shields were modelled after Deuchars' daughters and the one playing the bagpipes is said to be the best likeness.

Each animal carved on the armrests between the stalls is different. There are dogs, beavers, wild boars and even an elephant and a lion. To make corners meet, Talbot hounds are intertwining in the south-west turn of the stalls; each wooden panel on the wall resembles folded linen; the brass lamps are made up of an angel holding a light, the pelican – a medieval symbol for Christ's sacrifice – swings below and a heart finishing the chain.

The stone bosses on the ceiling – 57 of them in the ante-chapel and 98 in the main chapel – show leaves and fruit of plants and trees native to Scotland, and angels holding the coats of arms of early Knights and playing various musical instruments. The central bosses display saints and symbols important to the Order. The six central ones in the main chapel show, from west to east, the Royal Arms, St Giles, the badge of the Order of the Thistle, its patron St Andrew and the pelican.

The one symbol repeated over and over again is, of course, the thistle from which the Order takes its name. The thistle is the national flower of Scotland.

1 View of the Sovereign's stall
2 Memorial to Robert Lorimer, architect of the Thistle Chapel
3 Detail: cat and mouse
4 The interior of the Chapel facing east
5 The pelican boss
6 The angel with the bagpipes
7 Detail: brass angel on the door

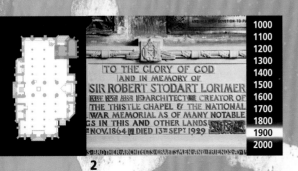

4

5

6

7

A CONCERT OF COLOURS – STAINED GLASS IN ST GILES'

The stained glass windows of St Giles' are possibly the most mesmerizing feature of the building. No matter if the sun is shining brightly or dark clouds are gathering over the Old Town, no matter if one looks at the Great East Window in the early morning hours with the sun illuminating the Resurrection, or at the north-facing windows in the subdued glow of the late afternoon – the light always seems to be just right for looking at these faces and stories in glass.

In comparison to the age of the building, these creations are fairly young – which is no surprise, looking at the history and implications of the Scottish Reformation. We do not know if the original glass windows of St Giles' were made to illustrate stories from the Bible. In the Middle Ages, when most people were not able to read the stories themselves, church windows often depicted important biblical scenes or told the lives of saints. From the very few pieces which were found in recent years we know only that the glass in St Giles' was certainly coloured. During the Reformation the decorated windows were removed and replaced by diamond-shaped panes of uncoloured glass. The few and small original glass pieces are now integrated into windows in the Lower Aisle.

The oldest windows we see in St Giles' today date from the Chambers' restoration in the 1870s and are along the northern and eastern walls of the Chancel. The succession of windows starting from the Chambers Aisle and reaching all the way to the steps to the Lower Aisle illustrates the life of Jesus. The whole sequence was made by the Ballantine family whose various members have, over the decades, created more than half the windows in St Giles'. In 1837, James Ballantine (1808–1877), who had started as a house painter and then studied art, founded a stained glass studio in Edinburgh. This was the first time that stained glass was made in Scotland after the Reformation. The family continued the stained glass business after his death.

Look out for the little boy reaching out of the Great East Window in the lower left-hand side corner. He is the only figure in the entire sequence of windows who seems to come out of

The Lower Aisle was created in 1982. It consists of several rooms located below the south-east corner of the Cathedral. It is now used as a restaurant.

1 Detail of the entrance porch
2 Medieval glass in the Lower Aisle
3 Three scenes from the Creation Cycle in the Lower Aisle
4 Sunlight on the Organ Window

the white glass frame. He reaches out with his arm as he tries to pull away from his mother. Many visitors interpret this as an invitation to join the congregation assembled around Jesus in the window.

The window to the left of the Great East Window shows the Last Supper with Judas Iscariot stealing out of the room; his hooded figure was not visible and only discovered a few years ago when all the windows were cleaned as part of the renewal of St Giles'. The next window to the left on the north wall, showing Christ's entry into Jerusalem, is dedicated to the memory of Robert Stevenson (1772–1850). The grandfather of Robert Louis Stevenson was a civil engineer working for the Northern Lighthouse Board. He designed 23 Scottish lighthouses, the most famous one situated on the Bell Rock off Arbroath on the East Coast of Scotland.

Since the 1870s the plain glass has been replaced – window by window – by the coloured glass we see today. Most of the windows are in memory of individuals with a connection to St Giles' or Edinburgh. A few of the outstanding windows in St Giles' are discussed separately in this book, but more windows and the artists who created them are described here.

The most modern glass is by the contemporary Edinburgh artist Christian Shaw (born in 1956) who designed the incredibly colourful window behind the organ, as well as six little glass images. These six panels show 'The Days of Creation' and are located in the Lower Aisle. They form a wonderful balance as the oldest (pre-Reformation) and some of the newest glass in St Giles' is placed almost side by side in this area of the building. The window behind the organ – made in 1991 – can never be seen in its entirety, so it is designed in a way to create patterns of light and colour on the walls, the floor and the organ case itself. These effects are best visible on a sunny day, and they alter dramatically with the time of the day and also throughout the year when the position of the sun on the horizon changes.

1 St Andrew as a bishop and as a fisherman
2 Nativity
3 A cherub from the Burne-Jones window
4 Kempe's 'signature' which he displayed on his windows
5 Detail from the North Window
6 The Last Supper
7 The Great East Window

Another outstanding Scottish artist who worked in St Giles' was Douglas Strachan. His masterpiece in the church is the North Window, but he also created some of the windows in the clerestory, as well as the one showing St Andrew in the Thistle Chapel. Strachan (1875–1950), born in Aberdeen, spent his early years working as a designer and drawing events and cartoons for newspapers. By persistent efforts, Strachan was eventually persuaded to work in glass and, in due course, became one of Scotland's leading stained glass artists.

The last Scottish artist to be discussed here is Daniel Cottier (1838–1891). Just one of the two windows he made for St Giles' survives, on the north wall between St Eloi Aisle and the Albany Aisle; it shows the allegorical figures of Faith, Hope, Charity, Truth, Justice and Mercy. The other one made by him was the Great West Window, entitled 'The Prophets', but the glass had deteriorated so badly that, in 1985, it was replaced with the Burns Window we see now. The original had been designed and put up in 1886, commissioned by a husband in memory of his wife who had died after childbirth when she was only 24. The plaque to her memory can still be seen on the wall below the new West Window.

Probably the best-known names of stained glass artists from England represented in St Giles' are William Morris (1834–1896) and Edward Burne-Jones (1833–1898). They produced one window for the church in 1886, showing 'The Crossing of Jordan' in the top panels and 'Ruth, Miriam and Jephthah's daughter' in the lower section. A thin line of clear glass separating it from the tracery makes the coloured glass seem to be almost levitating in the very substantial stone wall. The colours, especially the reds, are some of the most intense seen in any of the windows in the whole building.

7

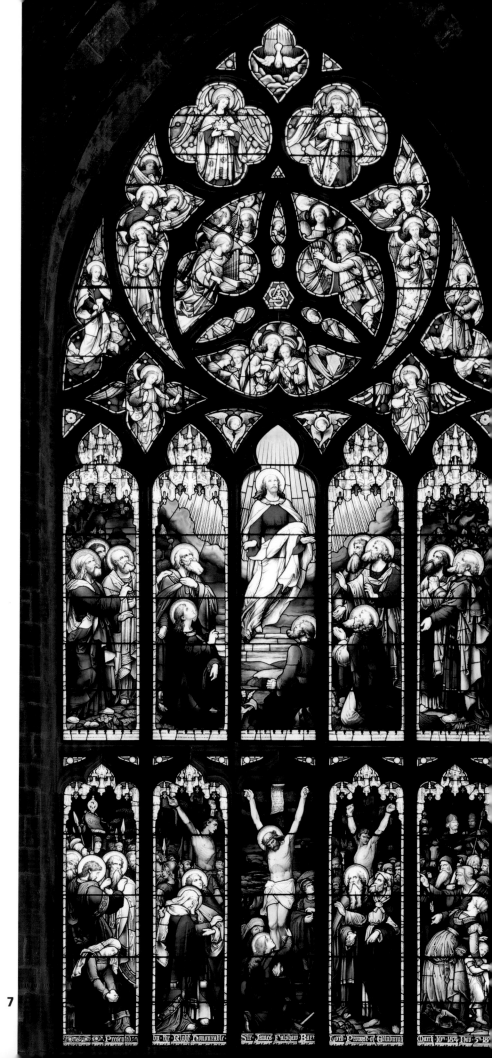

THE CHANCEL AND THE HOLY CROSS AISLE

The Chancel is, together with the Sanctuary, the oldest part of the building still standing today and the foundations and pillars date back to the early fourteenth century. The ceiling of this part of the building was raised in the 1460s to allow more light to come in through windows in the clerestory and there are some remarkable carvings up there. You have to look carefully because they are difficult to see, but all of them add to the story of St Giles'.

The boss at the very west of the Chancel for example – right above the painting of the coat of arms of George II, close to the Sanctuary – is a grotesque, a mask which dates back to the original Romanesque church, and was probably found and reused when the clerestory was built. That means it is almost 200 years older than the other bosses in the ceiling.

Almost too small to be seen from ground level, a little child's face hides in a flower-like boss further to the east. Further along still, two bosses are inscribed with IHS – the first three letters of the Greek name of Jesus – and with the beginning of the *Ave Maria* prayer – a clear pre-Reformation reference to the Virgin Mary.

The two most eastern arches of the Chancel also, like the clerestory, date from around 1460. If you look closely, the pillars look different and the arches are also slightly higher.

The last two pillars towards the east wall are decorated with heraldry, with four different coats of arms on each. All heraldic shields have a certain significance to the construction of this part of the church. Facing the Great East Window, the last pillar to the right is called the 'Town's Pillar'. On it are the arms of Edinburgh, of the bishop

1 The coat of arms of Sir Alexander Napier
2, 3 and **4** Coats of arms on the King's Pillar
5 Detail from the Elsie Inglis Memorial
6 Bosses on the Chancel ceiling
7 The Holy Cross Aisle

5

of St Andrews, of the vicar of St Giles', and of Sir William Preston, the donor of the arm bone of St Giles.

The last pillar on the left is called the 'King's Pillar'. It has the arms of King James II, his wife Mary of Gueldres, his son and heir King James III, and the fleur-de-lis, symbol of the King of France – Charles VII at the time. Looking at heraldic details of the arms of King James II, it is likely that he was dead by the time the shield went up. His son was King from 1460 to 1488.

The semi-pillar against the wall to the right of the Great East Window shows the coat of arms of Sir Alexander Napier of Merchiston, who made a large donation towards the church and was granted permission to decorate this pillar. The faces bordering the shield are not angels like the others, but clearly the head of a man and a woman. They are believed to be likenesses of Sir Alexander and Lady Napier.

The aisle separated off by an elaborate rail in the north-east corner of the church is called the Holy Cross Aisle. Today it is used for small services and ceremonies. It also contains a memorial to military chaplains and, each year, towards the end of May, a wreath is laid down at the spot.

Other memorials in this area are connected to medicine and one in particular reminds us of a fascinating woman – Elsie Inglis. Born in India in 1864, she studied at the Edinburgh School of Medicine for Women which was opened in 1886 by Dr Sophia Jex-Blake – also commemorated in St Giles' – and in Glasgow, becoming one of the first female doctors. She was also politically active and very much involved in the Scottish Federation of Women's Suffrage Societies. During the First World War, she was a pioneer in setting up field hospitals in France, Serbia and Russia and her name is still famous in these countries. She died from cancer in 1917 and her funeral was held in St Giles', where she had been a member of congregation.

FROM CHAMBERS AISLE TO ST ELOI AISLE

If you walk along beside the north wall from east to west, a small, intricate aisle comes into view, partly hidden behind a painted wooden screen which separates it from the main body of the church. The black and white tiled floor, the colourful Holy Table and the different plaques on the wall virtually invite one to step in and have a closer look at these little details.

This is the Chambers Aisle, which was restored on the site of the old vestry, built around 1500, and named in memory of William Chambers, the great restorer, in 1888. In the first half of the twentieth century, it also became known as the Chapel of Youth, forming the spiritual home of many local and national youth organisations. The silk banner on the west wall was Earl Haig's banner of the Order of the Bath which was given to St Giles' by his wife after his body had lain in state in the Cathedral. Earl Haig was senior commander of the British forces during the First World War.

Placed in front of the steps outside the Chambers Aisle are two bells. The smaller one is believed to be one of 23 music bells – a late-seventeenth-century carillon – from the tower. A set of them had played 'Why are you so sad on your wedding day' when the union of parliaments between England and Scotland took place. It is hung from a beam of wood which is said to have belonged to a ship of the Spanish armada.

The larger silver bell was the ship's bell of the HMS *Howe*, a King George V class battleship. After the ship was taken out of service in 1958, it was presented to St Giles'. Inside the bell is engraved the name of a girl who was baptised on board the ship. For that occasion the ship's bell would have been turned around, filled with water and the captain would have conducted the ceremony.

1 Detail of North Porch screen; the Masons
2 Detail of North Porch screen; the Hammermen
3 Detail of the Argyll memorial
4 Visiting the sick – one of the Acts of Mercy, detail from the pulpit
5 St Eloi
6 The Chambers Aisle
7 Nativity scene

Once you walk past the Chambers Aisle and the bells, you find yourself standing between two elaborate and detailed carvings: the pulpit and the North Porch screen. The pulpit was designed by William Hay, depicting the Acts of Mercy, and carved by John Rhind out of Caen stone in 1883. In 1888, John Rhind also carved the screen, decorating it with figures representing nine trades and their patron saints. In the Middle Ages various trade guilds supported altars in the church but those were destroyed during the Reformation. The Carpenters with St Joseph, the Masons with St John, the Hammermen (working with metal) with St Eloi and the Bakers with St Cuthbert are some of the trades depicted here. The coat of arms in the centre is that of William Chambers with the motto *Facta non verba* – Deeds not Words.

The centrepiece to St Eloi Aisle to the west of the screen is now a nineteenth-century monument to the Marquis of Argyll and a window to his supporters. The name of the aisle is taken from the saint of the hammermen, however. The hammermen supported an altar close to this spot and were one of the most influential guilds in the Middle Ages. Their symbol is set into the stone floor in nineteenth-century marble and mosaic and one of the carvings above shows the saint himself with a long beard, holding a goldsmith's hammer. The elaborate railing which closes off the aisle is by Francis Skidmore – as is much of the iron work in the building.

'I set the crown on the king's head,
He hastens me to a better crown than his own.'
Inscription on the Argyll Memorial

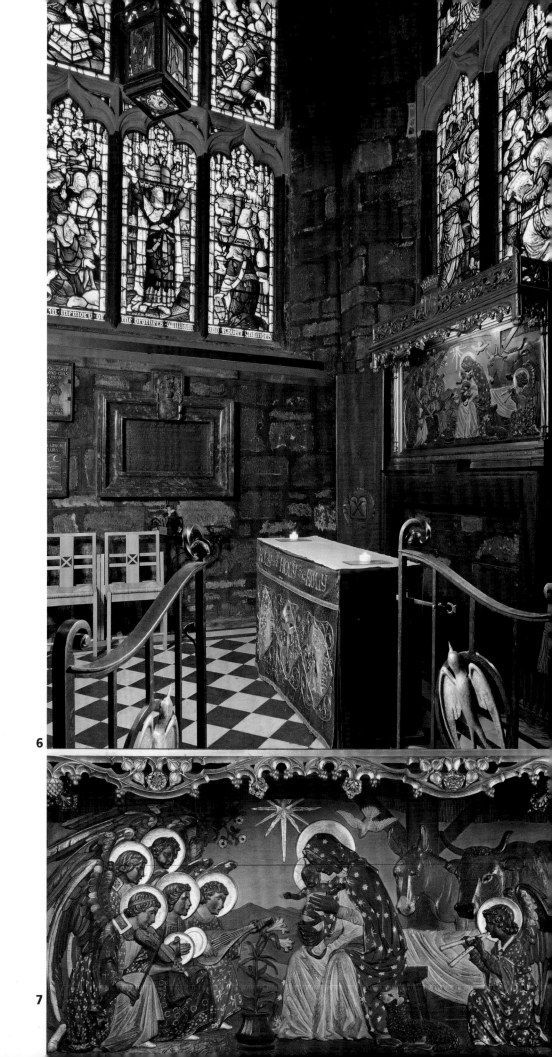

6

7

THE ALBANY AISLE

Located in the north-west corner is one of the oldest aisles in St Giles', the Albany Aisle. It was built in the very early fifteenth century and there are different suggestions as to why it was built.

The aisle takes its name from Robert, Duke of Albany. He was a brother to King Robert III, great-grandson to Robert the Bruce, and a powerful and highly influential man in his time. He seems to have taken a special interest in St Giles' and the role it played for the ambitiously growing Edinburgh. Robert III was a weak man in terms of ruling his country, as well as his physical condition. When David, the older of his two sons, was appointed as lieutenant of the kingdom, he was largely responsible to his uncle, Albany. After David became more and more defiant and failed to follow Albany's advice, he was imprisoned by him and his own father-in-law, Archibald, 4th Earl of Douglas. He died at Albany's palace in Falkland in 1402, but neither the Duke of Albany nor the Earl of Douglas was found guilty of his death, even though many people held them responsible. One suggestion is that they built the Albany Aisle out of remorse for their crime. The real reason why it was built will probably never be revealed: we only know that on the pillar supporting the aisle, the coats of arms of Albany and Douglas are displayed.

Today, the Albany Aisle commemorates those who lost their lives in the First and Second World Wars. It was refurbished as a war memorial chapel for private prayer and meditation during the late 1940s and dedicated in 1951. Looking closely at the lamp of remembrance, which was also lit in 1951, you will notice that its general shape resembles the St Giles' crown. The saltire and thistle are symbols for Scotland.

In the aisle are the two memorials to members of the congregation who lost their lives during the wars. The memorial on the west wall commemorates those killed in the First World War and the semi-circular recess in the north wall is carved with the names of those killed in the Second World War.

Other memorials in this aisle commemorate various Scottish and Lothian-based regiments and some tell heartbreaking stories.

1 **Detail from a Celtic cross**
2 **Coats of arms of the Earl of Douglas and of the Duke of Albany**
3 **St Michael the Archangel**
4 **The Albany Aisle**
5 **The Burne-Jones Window**

For example, the losses on the memorial to the 7th Royal Scots were not caused by enemy action but by the rail disaster of Gretna Green on 22 May 1915. This is still recorded as the worst rail disaster in British history. The soldiers were on their way to Liverpool to board a ship that was to take them to the Dardanelles to fight against the Turkish army. The train crashed into a locomotive, crushing the first three carriages. Just a few minutes later an express train, moving at high speed and running late, smashed into the wreckage and the derailed coaches instantly burst into flames. The heat was so great that only 83 bodies of the 227 dead soldiers were recognisable. Out of the entire battalion – 16 officers and 470 men – only 60 were able to continue the journey. When they reached their ship in Liverpool, the men were told to go back home. Maybe the disaster saved their lives – the battalion's final destination would have been Gallipoli. One of the officers killed in the train was Lieutenant Christian Salvesen, a member of the same family who donated the organ to St Giles' in 1992.

The 16th Royal Scots, or the 2nd City of Edinburgh Battalion, is called the Hearts Battalion. At the outbreak of the First World War, the entire Heart of Midlothian football team enlisted. Because the 16 men were under contract, they had to approach the club officials to allow them to break it. As the team had been tipped to have a very successful season, this was no small request, but the dedication to fight for King and country was so deep that they were given permission. Not even a third of the men returned from war.

The 17th Royal Scots Battalion – sponsored by Lord Rosebery – was sometimes called the Bantam Battalion because it was made up of men who were not tall enough to comply with the army regulation for height. They were not able to enlist in a 'normal' regiment until the government relaxed its rule. The fact that so many men did not reach the required height can be taken as a comment on the social situation of working-class and poor people in Britain in the early twentieth century.

INTO THE 21ST CENTURY

The main changes to St Giles' during the earlier part of the twentieth century included the building of the Thistle Chapel between 1909 and 1911, the installation of a new clock in the tower and the removal of the clock face from the outside in 1912, as well as various rearrangements of the furnishings of aisles and the conversion of the Albany Aisle into a war memorial chapel in 1951.

The 'Renewal of St Giles' started after the appointment of Gilleasbuig Macmillan as minister in 1973. There was a strong feeling that the interior of the church could be much improved and he and the well-known architect Bernard Feilden set out to put together a strategy for doing this. In his report from 1976, Feilden outlined what had to be done and fund-raising started the next year. By 1985, the first elements of the renewal had been accomplished, most noticeably the Sanctuary with the Holy Table had been established at the Crossing, the centre of the church, and special attention had been paid to partly retiling and

altering the floor levels. Also, the weathercock on the steeple – dangerously rocking after 300 years of overlooking the town – had been taken down, repaired and re-gilded and securely put up again. Below the south-east corner – under the Thistle Chapel and along the south aisles – the Lower Aisle was created, functioning as a meeting place as well as a small restaurant.

Over the next years, repairs to the roof, the stone walls and the tower continued. A new West Window in honour of Robert Burns was installed in 1985 and, in 1992, a new organ put in, generously donated by Alastair Salvesen.

In 1993, a new appeal for funds started, and, with a second phase of fund-raising from 1997 onwards, more work was carried out.

Repair work on the fabric continued slowly but steadily and, in 2005, all was finished, crowned by the placing of new gilded finials on the pinnacles of the spire. Since 2001, the stained glass had been taken out, cleaned and conserved. In 2005, all glass was

1 The Nave ceiling
2 Restoration work on a stone arch in 2009
3 The Lord and Lady Provost of Edinburgh leaving St Giles' Cathedral after a service.
4 The new lighting was put in place in 2009
5 The new porch by Leifur Breidfjord

1000
1100
1200
1300
1400
1500
1600
1700
1800
1900
2000

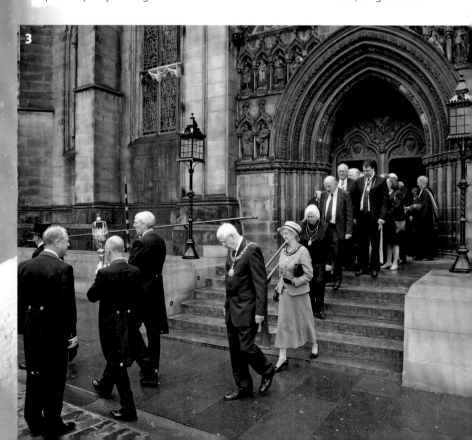

back in place and captivating visitors and worshippers alike with its newly regained vibrant colours.

More changes and improvements to the building which significantly altered the way it looks, have been carried out over the last few years. The cleaning of memorials and monuments and the painting of some of the plastered ceilings has already made the inside look much brighter than it has been for centuries, as will the cleaning of the interior stone and walls.

A completely new approach to the West Front was created with two ramps in addition to the centre steps outside and another ramp inside the building, making the church much more accessible.

During 2008 and 2009, a new lighting scheme was installed. Twenty-six chandeliers to brighten the aisles and ceilings, hidden spotlights under each window to illuminate the tracery and stonework, and fibre-optic lights in the old bell hole shining down on the Holy Table entirely transformed the appearance of the church. With settings for different times of the day, various services and special occasions, the lights might sometimes make the interior look like a mystic place of sheltered escape, at times like a cool, shadowy forest and, on occasion, like a warm haven of light.

The last addition to be completed by early 2010 was the new vestibule or porch at the inside of the main west entrance. The structure of dark metal screen and blue glass gives the Nave a new appearance, the vibrant colour changing in its effects throughout the day, when the light intensity varies. The new structure was designed by Leifur Breidfjord. The blue glass was painted in Germany and the metal screen was made in his home country, Iceland. The horizontal lines in the metal connect the porch with the window above, in which they are repeated. The window is also the work of Leifur Breidfjord.

4

5

THE ROBERT BURNS WINDOW

In 1985, a new window was installed in the west wall of St Giles', commemorating the poet Robert Burns (1759–1796). After years of negotiating over the requests for a memorial to him in the church, it was finally agreed to put in a window – and what a grand work of art it became.

Designed by the Icelandic artist, Leifur Breidfjord, it creates a very spiritual atmosphere as one looks westwards down the Nave. Abstract shapes, the change of light during the day and contemplative colours almost invite you to take a book with Burns' poetry and simply sit down and read.

Robert Burns' figure is visible on the glass in the lower centre section. His signature – taken from one of his last letters – is beneath it.

The lower part of the window, dominated by various shades of green, represents Burns' intimate knowledge of nature and his close relationship with the Scottish countryside, shaped by his life as a farmer. This influenced his poetry in a way that allowed him to put great, all-concerning concepts in the minutest and simplest surroundings, but also just to describe nature in words that paint all the colours right in front of your eyes.

Again rejoicing Nature sees
Her robe assume its vernal hues:
Her leafy locks wave in the breeze,
All freshly steep'd in morning dews.

The middle section, mainly coloured in shades of darker blue and purple, focuses on his ideas on community, common humanity and the circle of mankind: this circle shows on the glass, with glimpses of shapes that could represent a gathering of friends, hands reaching out, doves descending, a ladder of light ascending towards heaven, faces lifted towards the sky. The appeal of this window emerges most when you don't quite realise what you are seeing but lines of poetry somehow start floating through your mind.

The top of the window finally brings Burns' other passion into the picture – Love above all. The 'Red red rose', in a bright explosion of red and yellow, no different shades and hues this time – only one red and one yellow. The beams of the sun look as if they were made of ears of corn, forming a wonderful connection to the lower part of the window, which features the countryside.

The Icelandic artist Leifur Breidfjord (born in 1945) was given the commission for the window by the Burns Federation and the Kirk Session of St Giles' in 1983. His design is based on a careful and thorough study of Robert Burns' life and work and the themes also try to embrace concepts essential to Christianity. An additional challenge was that the glass had to fit into the existing nineteenth-century neo-Gothic frame and would be viewed from a great distance, but also from close up. The new window was made by the German company of W Derix of Rottweil and dedicated on 30 June 1985.

O, my luve's like a red, red rose,
That's newly sprung in June.
O, my luve's like the melodie,
That's sweetly play'd in tune.

Then let us pray that come it may,
(As come it will for a' that,)
That Sense and Worth,
o'er a' the earth,
Shall bear the gree, an' a' that.
For a' that, an' a' that,
It's coming yet for a' that,
That Man to Man, the world o'er,
Shall brothers be for a' that.

1000
1100
1200
1300
1400
1500
1600
1700
1800
1900
2000

VISITOR INFORMATION

SERVICES

St Giles' Cathedral has an active congregation with several hundred members.

There are several services on a Sunday, and additional acts of worship are conducted daily throughout the week.

VISITORS

The building is open to visitors throughout the year. Volunteer guides are on duty to answer questions and offer information.

Guided tours are available and should be booked in advance.

At the Information Desk, which is located inside the main entrance to the Cathedral, guidebooks, walk-round leaflets and photo permits can be purchased.

MUSIC AND ARTS

There are more than 100 free concerts in the Cathedral every year.

Every Sunday evening at 6pm, free concerts provide a stage for a wide range of musicians, appreciated by a faithful audience. On weekdays, musical performances at lunchtime, between noon and 1pm, invite casual visitors, as well as dedicated listeners, to sit down and escape the buzz of the town for a little while. These concerts are free, but donations are appreciated.

St Giles' also takes part in various festivals and hosts exhibitions and lectures.

SHOP

The adjacent Cathedral Shop offers a wide range of books, gifts and mementoes of the Cathedral and the Thistle Chapel.

To find out more about St Giles', the book *St Giles' – The Dramatic Story of a Great Church and its People* by Dr Rosalind K Marshall is recommended to gain a deeper insight into the history of the building.

CDs of the Cathedral Choir and Organ including *I was Glad: The Sound of Psalms, Hymns at St Giles'* or *The Organ at St Giles'* will provide a lasting sense of the unique atmosphere the Cathedral creates.

For more information and contact details please visit our website
www.stgilescathedral.org.uk

First published in 2010 by the Heritage House Group, Norfolk NR18 9RS.
Telephone 01603 813319 www.hhgroup.co.uk

Veronika Kallus: creative director and author

All photographs taken by Neil Jinkerson and are © of the Heritage House Group

Every effort has been made to trace all copyright holders, the publisher will be pleased to rectify any omissions in future editions.

Designed and produced by Heritage House Group
ISBN 978-0-85101-466-1
Printed in Great Britain A-81619-1/10